MW01519409

THE SUPERNATURAL

Since records were first kept, there have been tales about people with strange powers: people who are able to see into the future, to talk to the dead, to move things without touching them – even to fly. The majority of these people have proved to be fakes, but scientists have been unable to explain the behaviour of the remainder. In the following pages, we will look at some of these unusual powers that people have claimed to possess. After reading about them, decide for yourself whether these people have been tricking us or whether their abilities are genuine.

GREAT MYSTERIES

MYSTERIES

THE SUPERNATURAL

Rupert Matthews

Illustrated by Peter Dennis

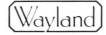

Wayland

Great Mysteries

Ancient Mysteries
Ghosts
Lands of Legend
Lost Treasures
Monster Mysteries
Sea Mysteries
The Supernatural
UFOs

Editor: David Cumming
Designer: Marilyn Clay
Cover illustration: A medium at work at the end of the last century.
Frontispiece: In the late 1800s, Douglas Home frequently astounded all his friends in London by flying around the room.

First published in 1989 by
Wayland (Publishers) Limited
61 Western Road, Hove
East Sussex BN3 1JD, England

Matthews, Rupert
  The supernatural.
  1. Supernatural
  I. Title II. Dennis, Peter, *1950 –*
  III. Series
  133

  ISBN 1–85210–460–0

Typeset by Lizzie George, Wayland
Printed in Italy by G. Canale & C.S.p.A., Turin
Bound in France by A..G.M.

Contents

Introduction

We live in a world where most things can be explained by scientists. They seem to have answers for most of our questions about the way the universe works.

However, many events occur which they cannot explain. For example it is absolutely impossible, according to our scientists, to predict what will happen in the future. Yet several people have escaped death because they have known that a ship or car in which they were due to travel would meet with a disaster.

Other people, called dowsers, are able to pin-point underground streams simply by walking across fields holding twigs in their hands. This ability has no scientific explanation – yet it happens.

Foretelling the future and dowsing are two

A fortune-teller at a seaside resort in Britain. Can she really predict the future from looking at the palms of your hands?

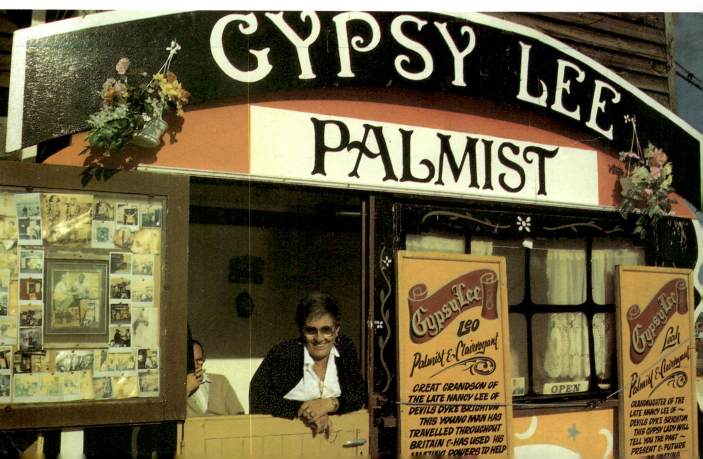

Punch's Spirit Lamp — Awful Explosion

examples of the supernatural. The supernatural is the word we use to describe all those events for which we have no explanation: we are unable to provide a reason for them happening. Most scientists prefer to ignore the supernatural. When a person claims to see into the future, scientists usually say that this is impossible and refuse to investigate it.

Many people feel that scientists are wrong to ignore supernatural events, especially as thousands of people claim to have experienced them. There is a lot of evidence to indicate that such things really do happen. Some people claim that all supernatural happenings can be linked together in a 'Goblin Universe'. This phrase was first used by Professor John Napier to describe events which occur, but which cannot be explained. Perhaps there is a single explanation for all supernatural events which has not yet been discovered.

In this book we shall look at some of the best-known types of supernatural activity, and discuss the evidence which seems to prove they occur. After reading about them, decide for yourself if our scientists are right or wrong in ignoring the supernatural. Should they take it more seriously?

A cartoon from the British Magazine Punch *in 1863 which pokes fun at the supernatural.*

These Americans have made a table levitate (fly) just by using the power of their minds. This was an experiment conducted in front of scientists in 1976.

Pope Pius's vision of victory

It is late afternoon on 7 October 1571. Pope Pius V is in his office in the Vatican in Rome, listening to one of his clerks telling him about what the Vatican has been spending its money on. It is a boring, but important task.

Suddenly the room seems to blur and vanish. Pius is startled to find himself looking at a mass of ships at sea. Some of them carry flags of Christian countries; others fly the colours of the Muslim Turkish Empire. As Pius watches, the ships rush at each other, their oars gleaming in the sunlight. Pius can see canon firing and ships burning, but he can hear nothing.

The clerk can see nothing unusual, but notices that the Pope is no longer listening to him. Suddenly, Pius turns around. 'Leave all this,' he says, 'we must give thanks to God. Victory has been won by the Christian fleet.'

Two weeks later, a messenger gallops into the Vatican. He carries important information for the Pope. A great naval victory has been won at Lepanto. The Christian fleet has defeated the Turkish one. The battle took place on the afternoon of 7 October.

Mind power

Some of the commonest supernatural abilities seem to be concerned with the human mind. They are known to researchers as Extra Sensory Perception (ESP) and Telekinesis (TK). ESP is the ability to be aware of something without using the normal senses of sight, hearing, taste, smell or touch. TK involves the ability to move an object simply by thinking, and without touching it.

Many instances of ESP have been recorded. Some, such as the vision of Pius V, concern great events and have become famous. Others are equally exciting but concern less important happenings. In 1827, for example, a British woman, Maria Marten, eloped from her Suffolk home with a man named William Corder. Some time later, Maria's mother dreamt that her daughter was dead and buried in a red barn. After much searching, the woman found the barn seen in her dream and ordered the floor to be dug up. The body of Maria Marten was found in

In 1986 an American, W E Cox, blew up a balloon in front of scientists after it had been placed in a sealed box. The scientists found no evidence of trickery. This is an example of telekinesis.

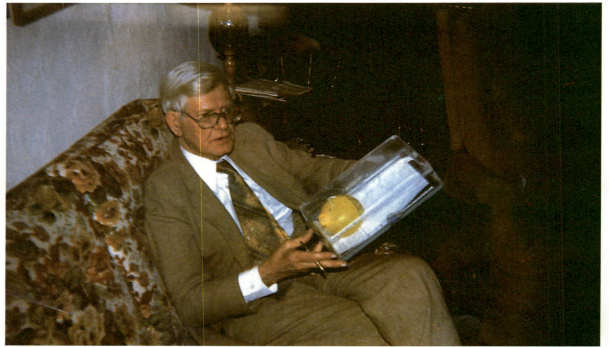

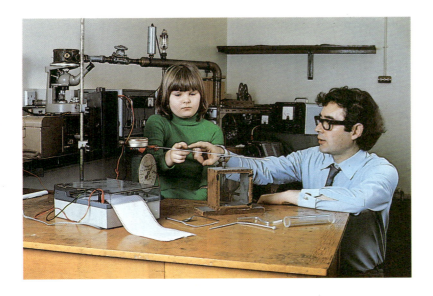

A scientist carrying out tests on an 8-year-old girl who can bend pieces of metal with just the slightest touch.

the corner. William Corder was arrested and confessed to her murder.

In most cases of ESP, the person who receives a message suddenly 'sees' a scene which is happening far away. The person has no control over the event and cannot explain it. It simply happens.

A few people, however, seem to have control over their ESP. They are known as clairvoyants or psychics. Sometimes the powers of clairvoyants can be very helpful. In 1978 a Los Angeles schoolboy vanished. A local psychic promptly drew a picture of a man she felt had murdered him. The picture was shown to the boy's family who recognized it as that of a neighbour. The man was arrested and confessed to the murder.

Unfortunately, the statements of clairvoyants are either wrong or vague far more often than they are correct. For instance, during a police hunt for a murderer in Britain, one clairvoyant accurately described the man, but dozens of others produced descriptions which were totally wrong.

Researchers investigating ESP cannot simply wait for a vision to come and then investigate it. Instead they invent tests which, they hope, will reveal ESP powers. Perhaps the most common of these is for one person to draw a picture. The clairvoyant is then asked to reproduce the picture, without having seen it.

Dozing for ESP

Most ESP visions occur when a person is dozing or resting. As a result, many people say ESP is only a dream.

Stanislawa Tomczyk making a plate hover above her kitchen table by focusing her powers of thought on it.

One of the earliest investigators to use this technique was Upton Sinclair. He sketched pictures which his wife, a psychic, then attempted to reproduce. On a staggering 76 out of every 100 occasions, Mrs Sinclair produced a similar picture to that drawn by her husband.

Even more dramatic than ESP is telekinesis. This word means 'distant movement' and involves the ability to move objects without touching them. Such 'brain power' is extremely rare.

In 1912, a Polish woman, Stanislawa Tomczyk, found she could make objects fly through the air by concentrating her powers of thought on to them. However, she had no control over the movements. Some fifty years later, a Russian woman, Nina Kulangina, claimed to be able to move things without touching them. She was able to move pens, stop pendulums and even move three objects at once. Despite strict tests, no sign of trickery was ever discovered.

The best-known person to claim TK powers is an

The Swiss table rocker

In 1853 Count Agenor de Gasparin of Switzerland investigated seances at which tables rocked and turned. He decided that the brain power of the people at the seance was responsible for this, and not the spirits of the dead. This early suggestion of TK was largely ignored.

Israeli named Uri Geller. Geller shot to fame in June 1972 when a German reporter suggested that he do something spectacular to prove his powers. He asked Geller to stop a cable-car in mid-journey. Geller and a group of reporters drove to a cable-car station. Geller began to concentrate and minutes later the cable-car halted.

Over the following years, Geller appeared on stage and on television in many countries. On every occasion he managed to produce some amazing TK effect. Perhaps the most common was his famous 'spoon bending'. Taking a metal spoon in his left hand, Geller would gently stroke it until it bent. No evidence of trickery could be found by researchers. Several magicians said they could repeat Geller's activities, but they failed to do so when they were put to the test. The astounding powers of Geller have never been disproved or explained.

Uri Geller, probably the most famous person to claim that he has powers of telekinesis. His ability to bend spoons and stop watches has never been disproved or even explained.

13

Did author foretell sinking of the *Titanic*?

It is the evening of 14 April 1912. The luxurious liner *Titanic* is slowly settling in the water. Her hull has been ripped open by an iceberg. Men and women are struggling to escape from the doomed ship, but there are not enough lifeboats to hold all of them. Hundreds of people know that they are going to die unless help arrives quickly.

Lifeboats, crowded with women and children, push out from the *Titanic*. Wives part from husbands for the last time. On the decks the dance band continues to play popular tunes as the water slowly rises. No help arrives before the ship sinks and 1,513 people die.

In one of the lifeboats sits a woman who cannot believe what has happened. She only recently read a novel by Morgan Robertson in which a ship named *Titan* sinks after striking an iceberg. In the book the fictional ship is the same size and carries the same number of passengers as the *Titanic*. The ship also sinks in exactly the same area of the Atlantic Ocean as the *Titanic*. How could Robertson have produced such an accurate description of the disaster before it occurred?

Glimpsing the future

The similarities between the imaginary *Titan* and the real-life *Titanic* seem truly extraordinary. However, sceptics point out that it could be nothing more than coincidence. The author, Morgan Robertson, might have used the idea without realizing that he was predicting the disaster. Other predictions cannot be dismissed so easily. They foretell incidents which seem highly unlikely.

On 3 May 1812, a British man dreamt that he saw the prime minister, Spencer Perceval, murdered in the lobby of the House of Commons in London. Perceval was dressed in blue and his attacker in brown. Eight days later, Spencer Perceval was shot by a man wearing a brown coat, while he himself was dressed in blue.

A more recent example of premonition happened in April 1974 when a visitor to the Tower of London heard the screams of young children. A few weeks later a terrorist bomb wounded more than a dozen children at the same spot.

The main difficulty in investigating premonitions is that they are often not recognized as such until after the event they predict. John Dunne, for instance, dreamt about a train being derailed at a certain spot in Scotland. It was only after a train accident at that spot that Dunne realized he had experienced a premonition.

Under such circumstances, it is almost impossible for researchers to be certain whether or not they are dealing with a true premonition. The witness might simply have linked a dream with a

The prophet who was wrong

In 1925 an Indian holy man, called Krishnamurti, convinced his followers that the Second Coming of Christ would occur in Sydney, Australia. He persuaded them to build a 2,000 seat stand so that they could watch the great event in comfort. After four years nothing had happened, so the stand was demolished.

similar event when there was nothing but
coincidence to link the two. Other people might claim
to have premonitions simply to become famous.

An important investigation into premonitions
revealed these problems. On 21 October 1966 a
huge coal-tip collapsed on to the Welsh village of
Aberfan, killing 140 persons. Many people claimed
that they had foreseen the tragedy. Dr John Barker,
a psychiatrist, decided to investigate.

Barker questioned seventy-six of them. Some of
their predictions were rather vague. One person
dreamt that the village school had vanished, and it
was, indeed, destroyed by the tip. A few days before
the event, one person killed in the disaster had told
her mother that her death was approaching.
Though it could not be proved that any of the
premonitions had occurred before the disaster,
Barker noticed some interesting points. None of the
premonitions had predicted the entire tragedy, only
parts of it. Also, the premonitions began about three

*In 1812, a British man's
dream about the prime
minister being
assassinated turned out to
be true – or was it pure
coincidence?*

weeks in advance and were most common the day
before the disaster. Such a pattern occurs in other
studies of premonitions.

Some people seem able to predict the future
almost at will. The best known of them is
Nostradamus, a Frenchman born in 1503. In the
course of his life Nostradamus made several
remarkable predictions. He once stopped an
unimportant monk and told him that he would be
made pope. Many years later the monk actually did
become pope.

In later life, Nostradamus collected his
predictions together in a series of books. Some
were predictions he claimed had already come true;

*The scene at the Welsh
town of Aberfan on 21
October 1966 after a
coal-tip had slid down on
to it, killing 140 adults
and children. Many people
in Aberfan claimed to
have foreseen the disaster.*

18

The lucky student

On 8 March 1946 John Godley, a student at Oxford University, had a strange dream, in which he saw the names of two racehorses. On waking, Godley found that they were running in races that day. He promptly bet on them, and both won. Over the following twelve years, Godley had many similar dreams and won a lot of money.

others concerned the future. These writings were in verse, and often used complicated imagery. They are, therefore, difficult to understand accurately. For instance, one verse reads: 'Near the harbour and in two cities will be two scourges the like of which have never been seen'. Some people believe this predicts the atomic bombs dropped on the Japanese cities of Hiroshima and Nagasaki, both large ports, in 1945. Others point out that the 'prediction' is so vague that it could mean almost anything.

Perhaps the most remarkable prophet of all is not even known by name. He was a Frenchman captured by German soldiers during the First World War (1914–18). He predicted that Germany would

Oxford Univeristy student John Godley won a lot of money in the 1940s after seeing the winners of horse races in his dreams.

Nostradamus (1503–66), the French doctor and astrologer. His book of predictions, written in verse, is still read by people all over the world.

lose the war and that afterwards there would be so much money that people would not bother to pick it up in the streets. In 1932, he continued, a tyrant would come to power in Germany and a war would begin in 1939. Germany would lose this war, the man predicted, and be occupied by foreign soldiers. All these things came true. Germany did lose the First World War, after which inflation made money almost worthless. Hitler gained power in 1933, only one year after the predicted date, governed like a tyrant and led Germany to defeat in the Second World War (1939–45).

The unhappy prophetess

According to ancient Greek legends, Cassandra was given the gift of prophecy by the gods. Unfortunately, no one ever believed her predictions and the people she tried to protect always rushed headlong to their deaths.

Cassandra, the Greek prophetess, whose predictions were ignored, resulting in the death of many people.

How do people like this unknown Frenchman, see the future so accurately? Perhaps more disturbing is the thought that the future is already decided and that nothing we can do will change it.

A helping hand from beyond the grave

It is March 1978. Luiz Gasparetto has travelled from Brazil to London to appear on a BBC television programme. He sits at a table with paper, pen and crayons in front of him. The studio lights are switched on and the cameras zoom in on Gasparetto.

The presenter introduces Gasparetto to the audience. Almost at once he enters a trance and picks up a pen. He begins to draw. Gasparetto's hand flies across the paper, producing a picture in a modern style. He suddenly snatches a crayon in his other hand and starts sketching on another sheet of paper. He is producing two pieces of art at the same time. No sooner is one picture finished than Gasparetto starts another. The amazing display goes on throughout the television programme. In little more than an hour, Gasparetto produces twenty-one pictures.

They are shown to art experts who can identify the styles of many famous artists, all of whom are dead. Gasparetto claims that his hands are being guided by the spirits of dead artists who communicate with him.

Talking to the dead

Above *An invitation to one of Florrie Cook's seances.*

Below *Many mediums have proved to be fakes. This picture shows the tricks one used to persuade people he was in touch with the dead.*

Death is the end of life. However, most religions teach that the soul (or the spirit, as it is often called) survives in some way. If the soul continues to exist, some people believe it might be possible to communicate with the dead. In the 1850s people began saying that they were in contact with spirits. These people became known as mediums. They held seances during which many people became convinced that they were in touch with dead friends and relatives. Within a few years the spiritualist movement, as it became known, had attracted many followers in Europe and America.

Most people, however, remained sceptical. It seemed that some mediums were genuine, but others were suspected of trickery. Then, in 1874, the medium Florrie Cook agreed to a series of scientific tests. These were carried out by the highly respected British scientist, Sir William Crookes.

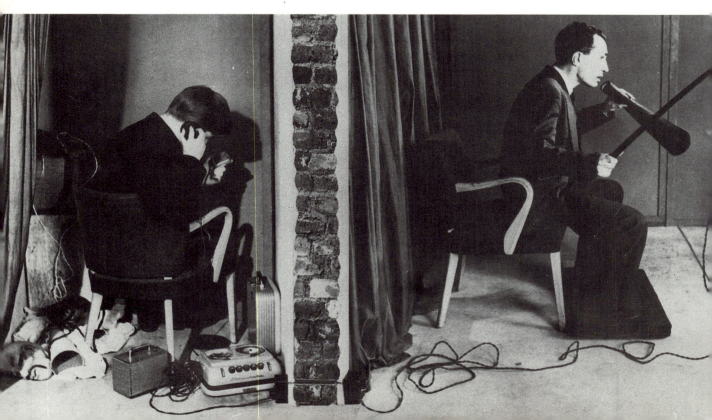

Florrie Cook claimed that she was able to materialize a spirit, named Katie King, who was in contact with other spirits. Over a period of several months, Crookes attended many of Florrie's seances. He became convinced that he was witnessing a genuine contact with dead people.

After the end of the First World War in 1918, there was a great increase in interest in spiritualism. Hundreds of thousands of young men had been killed in the fighting and their families and friends were eager to believe that they could get in touch with them.

Unfortunately many dishonest people pretended to be mediums simply to make money. They would charge for seances and trick their customers into thinking that they were in touch with the spirits of dead relatives. The mediums made it seem as if the spirits moved tables and rapped out coded messages. Such 'mediums' would talk to their customers before a seance and skillfully find out whose spirit they wanted to contact. Then, during

Frederick Bond, a British archaeologist, said he was helped in his work by the ghost of a dead monk. With his guidance, Bond made many important discoveries, but few people believed him. Do you?

In 1907 the excavation of Glastonbury Abbey in Britain was entrusted to Frederick Bond, a well-known archaeologist. Bond was interested in mediums, and was pleasantly surprised when the spirit of a long-dead monk made contact with him. Under his guidance Bond made many important discoveries. However, as soon as the source of his information was discovered, Bond was dismissed and forbidden ever again to set foot in the abbey. He died in poverty many years later.

the seance, the 'medium' would pretend to receive messages from these spirits.

It has been estimated that in America alone these 'mediums' earned $125 million in a single year. The exposure of these 'spook crooks', as they became known, convinced many people that spiritualism itself was nothing but fakery.

In recent years, however, spiritualism has been taken more seriously. Many researchers feel that there are honest mediums who are able to communicate with the dead. Perhaps the most famous of recent mediums was the British woman, Doris Stokes. She said that she was in touch with the spirits of friends and relatives of people who attended her meetings. She told them that she could hear voices which asked her to pass on messages and advice. The fact that Mrs Stokes was able to reveal facts she could not have known herself convinced many that she was truly in touch with the dead.

However, other mediums seem to be able to produce even more startling effects. These mediums are so-called psychic artists who produce works claimed to be inspired by long-dead artists.

One of the best known of these is another British woman, Rosemary Brown. Mrs Brown had already had experiences of ESP (see page 10) when, in 1964, she claimed to have been confronted by the figure of Franz Liszt, the famous Hungarian composer who died in 1886. Liszt, she said, began dictating music to her which he had composed after his death. Liszt was joined by other composers, including Beethoven, Chopin and Brahms.

Doris Stokes, a well-known British medium. She used to hold large meetings where she would pass messages from dead relatives to people in the audience.

Without doubt, the music written down by Mrs Brown is in the style of the great composers, but few people accept her story. At first it was suggested that Mrs Brown might be producing the music herself. But it was soon found that she was not a good pianist and was quite unable to understand the more complicated musical works she wrote. The truth of Rosemary Brown's claims has not been proved.

The same lack of convincing proof applies to the case of Matthew Manning, who produces dozens of paintings, claiming that they are inspired by dead artists. Manning says that all he needs to do is sit with a pen and paper in front of him. Soon an artist will start to direct his hand to produce a picture.

The gift of communicating with the dead is claimed by many people. Some seem more convincing than others. The mediums may quote facts or messages which it seems unlikely they would know themselves. However, it has never been proved that these facts come from the dead.

Rosemary Brown claims that dead composers, like Beethoven and Liszt, dictate music to her.

The flying monk of Copertino

The sun shines through the windows of the chapel on this Sunday morning. Mass has been said by the abbot. Now he leads the monks of Copertino, Italy, in prayer. With heads bowed, the monks intone the words.

The abbot glances up to check that all is well with his congregation. His voice halts in mid-speech. His mouth falls open in shock and surprise. Joseph, one of the junior monks, is floating through the air. Still deep in prayer, Joseph is obviously unaware that he is flying.

Noticing that the abbot has stopped reciting, the monks look up. They too see Joseph floating towards the altar. Some monks leap to their feet in surprise, others faint. Alerted by the noise, Joseph opens his eyes. He does not seem at all surprised to find himself some metres in the air. He gently floats down to the floor.

The superhumans

Colin Evans levitating at a spiritualist meeting in London in 1938.

Below *This Hindu worshipper in Malaysia can feel no pain, even though both his cheeks are pierced by a steel rod.*

There are a few individuals who claim to perform feats which would be impossible for most of us. Very often their claims are supported by careful investigation. Even so, scientists still dismiss their behaviour as trickery or exaggeration. However, there is increasing evidence that some people can defy the laws of nature.

Possibly the most amazing form of unusual behaviour is the ability to fly, or levitation as it is known. The young Italian monk who levitated at mass in Copertino was a simple peasant boy named Joseph. Born in 1603, Joseph was deeply religious and became a monk at the age of 22. Whenever he became excited, particularly when at prayer, Joseph would float upwards. Many highly respected people including noblemen and Pope Urban VIII, witnessed his flights. Joseph's sincere religious beliefs were given as the reason for his remarkable gift. After his death, Joseph was created a saint.

In the late 1800s, another man achieved fame through his ability to float through the air. Douglas Home mixed with important people in Britain and was always happy to show his peculiar skills. He

could cause musical instruments to play without touching them and could create winds. But most spectacular was his gift of flight. Home often floated through the air, drifting in and out of windows at will. He continued to do this for nearly twenty-five years from 1855 onwards. Though often investigated by scientists, Home was never shown to be cheating or using hidden machinery.

More recent examples of levitation come from India and China. In 1936 a group of Europeans watched an Indian holy man float above the ground. Many European travellers to Tibet, in China, have reported seeing holy men flying through the air.

Another unusual activity performed by Indian holy men is firewalking. This was first seen in 1912 in India, but today it is most common on Pacific islands, such as Fiji and Bali. Usually a pit is dug and filled with wood and stones. The wood is then set on fire and allowed to burn until it is reduced to white-hot embers. The embers are then raked off, leaving the stones at a temperature of about 500°C. The firewalkers then stroll across the stones as if they were quite cool.

Researchers who have investigated firewalking have noticed several features. No trickery, in the form of shoes or other protection, can be found. However, most firewalkers spend many hours, sometimes days, preparing themselves. They pray, fast and meditate for long periods of time. It has been suggested that the walkers are in some kind of trance, but this does not explain why they are not burnt by the hot stones.

Some people seem naturally immune to fire. One such man was Nathan Coker, an American blacksmith of the last century. He was able to pick

This picture, from the Petit Journal *magazine of 1908, shows southern Indians walking on hot coals during a religious ceremony.*

up red-hot pieces of iron, straight from the fire, without burning his hands.

More shocking for those who meet them are the people who seem highly charged with electricity. In 1952, for instance, a Welshman named Brian Williams found he could cause an electric light bulb to glow simply by stroking it with his hand. Less useful was the gift of Brian Clements. For a time in 1967 he found that he gave electric shocks to anybody who touched him.

Other people have been known to be 'magnetic'. In 1890 Louis Hamburger found that pins, pen nibs and other metal objects stuck to his hands. A stronger attraction was generated by Mrs Timmer who, in 1938, showed she could lift cutlery and fairly heavy pieces of metal simply by touching them with her fingers.

But perhaps the most astonishing of all the

Nathan Coker, the American blacksmith, who could pick up a red-hot horse-shoe from the fire without burning himself.

Louis Hamburger was a 'magnetic' person, who found that all sorts of metal objects stuck to him.

superhuman gifts is the one which enables life to continue when starved of air. The gift has been claimed by many Indian holy men, one of the earliest of whom was named Hadridas. In 1835 Hadridas agreed to a test. He spent many days fasting and preparing for the ordeal. Then Hadridas sat down, closed his eyes and stopped breathing. His pulse also ceased. He was then placed in a chest and buried. Guards were placed around the spot to ensure no trickery was involved. More than a month later, Hadridas was dug up. Within seconds he was on his feet and asking for a meal.

Most of these stories of extraordinary human behaviour are not taken seriously. It is said that either the whole thing was a trick or that the witness was exaggerating what had happened. This explanation would be believable if only one or two examples of levitation or firewalking existed. However, dozens of witnesses claim to have seen such events. Perhaps some humans are able to achieve what seems impossible.

Uncovering a deadly mine in wartime

The small patrol pushes slowly through the Vietnamese jungle. It is 1969 and the five American soldiers are part of a large army helping South Vietnam defend itself against North Vietnam. The soldiers tread carefully. Each bush might hide an enemy soldier or a booby trap.

The patrol is led by Sergeant Davis, who is holding two pieces of wire lightly in front of him. As Davis creeps forward he stares intently at the wires. Suddenly they twitch and swivel apart. Davis raises his arm to stop the patrol, then drops to his knees. He digs carefully in the soil and uncovers a deadly mine. He gently removes the explosive device. Then he stands up, holds the wires in front of him and walks forward again.

Davis had been shown how to locate mines by dowsing by another soldier a few weeks earlier. He does not know how the process operates, but the army is short of proper mine detectors. The dowsing system has saved Davis's life dozens of times.

Tapping the force

For centuries some people have claimed to locate hidden objects by a process so bizarre that it has been dismissed as impossible by scientists. These people are called dowsers, who can find underground objects simply by walking across the ground holding a stick, pieces of wire or a pendulum. If what they are holding twitches, the object is immediately underfoot. No one can explain why this happens.

One of the earliest references to dowsing comes from Germany in 1556, when miners used it to find coal. But proper records on dowsing were not kept until the last century. These writings mention a very famous dowser, a British man named John Mullins. On one occasion a Yorkshire farmer asked Mullins to find water on his land. Mullins arrived and then

John Mullins dowsing for water on a farmer's land in the nineteenth century. He discovered an underground stream no one had known about.

walked across a field with his dowsing stick in his hand. After only a few minutes he stopped and began to dig. As the astonished farmer looked on, Mullin's spade uncovered an underground stream nobody had known about.

During the early years of this century dowsing became increasingly popular, and dowsers realized that objects other than water could be found. An American engineer discovered that he could locate electricity cables through concrete floors. With practice, he could also tell if the cables were damaged. This gift helped him in his job and reduced repair costs.

Skilled dowsers appear to be able to find almost anything. All the dowser needs to do is concentrate on that object for the rod or pendulum to react to it when it comes in range. Cracked pipes, gold and gas mains have all been located by dowsers.

About fifty years ago, some dowsers realized that they were reacting to signals which did not seem to indicate any object in the ground beneath them. More puzzling was the fact that, if the places where the dowsers had felt the reactions were plotted on a map, the points formed a straight line. What were these mysterious lines?

The answer proved to be every bit as mysterious and controversial as the dowsing itself. In 1921 Alfred Watkins, a British business man, noticed that

A seventeenth-century picture showing the different ways of holding a dowsing rod.

A British man dowsing for water in Cornwall with the help of two metal rods.

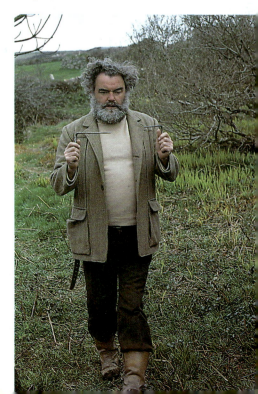

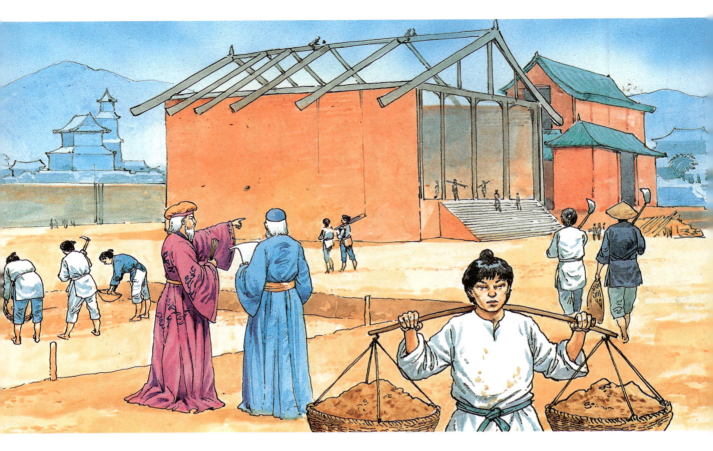

Two Chinese geomancers checking that a new building has been positioned correctly on a 'dragon path', which is the same as a ley line.

several ancient sites near his home lay on a straight line. Watkins consulted a map and discovered that he could recognize several other such alignments, or 'ley lines' as he called them.

A ley line is a straight line on which a number of ancient sites are to be found. These sites include stone circles, such as Stonehenge, prehistoric burial mounds, holy wells, ancient earthworks and churches. The structures themselves do not need to be very old. Many modern churches are built on sites which have been used for centuries. Watkins, and others, have found hundreds of these ley lines

The path of the dragon

In China the existence of lines of earth power, known as dragon paths, has long been accepted. In ancient China, the geomancers, who discovered dragon paths, were very important people. Whenever a new building was to be erected, the dragon paths were checked to ensure that the site was favourable. It was believed that if a building was built in the wrong place, it could upset the flow of the earth power.

running across Britain and Europe. Most ley lines are about 15 kilometres long, though some are much shorter and others are longer.

Archaeologists do not believe that these lines exist at all. They say that the straight lines are produced by chance. If a number of sites, say schools, are chosen at random, some of them will always lie on straight lines. However, efforts to show that ley lines happen by chance are not convincing. It has been estimated that the chance of a ley line occurring is about 1 in 1,000, yet they actually occur far more often than this.

Exactly what ley lines are is not clear. Watkins thought that they marked a trade route. Other investigators, particularly dowsers, have been more adventurous in their ideas. It has been suggested that the lines are channels for an 'earth power'. This earth power is said to originate within our planet and to run across the surface along ley lines.

It is this power which the dowsers claim to detect. It is said that prehistoric humans could detect this energy and built their stone circles and burial mounds on them.

Evidence for this earth power is still weak. It depends largely on the findings of dowsers, who are not really sure what they are sensing, nor how they sense it. Although it seems certain that dowsers can locate many things, their claims of finding earth power lines still remains in doubt. If such a force really does exist, there should be a scientific explanation to account for it. Perhaps such an explanation could be found if only scientists would take the matter seriously.

A picture showing a ley line connecting up several ancient sites in the British countryside.

The black streams

Some dowsers believe that the earth power lines which they discover may be good or evil. The evil lines are known as black streams. During the 1970s, a British farmer noticed that his new farm was upsetting him and that his livestock were often ill. He called in a dowser, who discovered a black stream running across the land. The dowser hammered iron stakes into the ground because they would block the stream. After this, the farmer felt happier and his animals became healthier.

Ibrahim returns in someone else's body

Young Imad Elawar steps down from the car. He has been driven to the village of Khirby in Lebanon, a place he has never visited before. He runs across the village street to a house. Then he turns to Ian Stevenson, a British scientist. 'This is where I lived with Jamile,' he says. Imad then describes the interior of the house, though he has never entered it. Stevenson knocks on the door and asks to be shown around. The house is exactly as Imad described.

Imad then goes to the next house. He calls the owner by name and treats him as if they were old friends. Imad then says that his real name is Ibrahim Bouhamzy and that he has lived in Khirby for many years. Stevenson discovers that a man named Ibrahim Bouhamzy had lived in Khirby and died thirteen years earlier.

In the course of his visit, Imad recognizes many friends of Ibrahim and describes how he died. He is even able to describe the personal possessions of the dead Ibrahim. Onlookers are convinced that Ibrahim has returned to life in the body of Imad Elawar.

Living more than once

The Eastern religions of Buddhism and Hinduism, and some followers of Islam, teach that the soul is reborn on earth after death. This process is known as reincarnation. In Western countries especially, scientists have not yet accepted that humans have souls which survive death. Yet there is a surprising amount of evidence which seems to indicate that reincarnation does occur, both in Eastern and Western countries, and that it is not uncommon.

In recent years, evidence in favour of reincarnation has begun to emerge in Europe and America. The sensation of *déjà vu* has long been known. This occurs when a person visits a place they do not know and feels that they have been

A girl being hypnotized to see if she can recall a past life.

there before. Such feelings might be caused by memories of a past life. They have, however, been dismissed as figments of the imagination.

More important is the case of a French art student named Diane, which was reported in the 1960s. In her early twenties, Diane remembered sailing to the Pacific as a young child on a ship named *Chandernagor*. Diane claimed that the voyage ended in disaster with many passengers being eaten by cannibals. She had, however, never made such a voyage. Diane's teacher investigated and found that Diane was remembering a true voyage which took place in 1879, years before she had been born. Researchers became convinced that Diane was recalling the event from a past life.

In the 1970s, Arnall Bloxham, a British hypnotist, revealed staggering new evidence for reincarnation. Bloxham used his hypnotic powers to take patients back to their youth. One day Bloxham asked a patient to remember what had happened before their birth. To Bloxham's amazement, the patient began describing a life which had taken place many years earlier. Bloxham felt certain he had stumbled on evidence for reincarnation.

Bloxham hypnotized hundreds of people and asked them to remember events before their birth. Most recalled past lives which they described in great detail. Bloxham taped their conversations and began to investigate the details. The vast majority of the lives were very ordinary. One subject said she had been a seamstress in London during the eighteenth century.

Bloxham found it impossible to discover if these

Followers of Buddhism, like this monk in Thailand, believe that we are reborn on earth after death.

people had really existed or not. Birth certificates and other records were only introduced in recent years. However, he was able to match the descriptions of everyday life with reality. Almost without exception, Bloxham found his subjects were accurately describing life in past centuries. A few subjects, however, mentioned historical characters in their past lives. When these statements could be compared with the truth, they were found to be accurate.

When Bloxham published his findings, other

In the 1970s, a woman in Brazil remembered being murdered in Europe by a German soldier during the Second World War (1939–45).

44

hypnotists began similar research. Perhaps the most remarkable research programme was that undertaken by the American Helen Wambach. She hypnotized as many as sixty people at a time and asked them specific questions about past lives. The subjects were asked to write down the answers. Wambach has found that most people were able to recall past lives. In the vast majority of cases, the information remembered proved to be accurate.

These astounding results seemed to present evidence of reincarnation, but it was not long before doubts were being cast upon the findings. Scientists, who did not accept that reincarnation was possible, inspected the stories of past lives. In many cases they found that the subject had read about the historical period in question and revealed the information under hypnosis.

One of the most famous of Bloxham's cases involved a woman who recalled six lives. The historical knowledge shown by the woman was remarkable. It was found, however, that the 'past lives' were nothing more than descriptions of historical novels. The woman must have read the books and forgotten them and then 'recalled' the tales as past lives.

The scientists concluded that there was no evidence in the hypnotic sessions to prove reincarnation. They decided that the so-called 'past lives' came from deep within a person's imagination.

The scientists' conclusions do not account for all cases of past lives revealed under hypnosis. Even if all the cases could be explained away, the evidence of Diane and Imad Elawar and other similar cases would still remain. Perhaps there is, indeed, the possibility of reincarnation.

Conclusion

It is impossible to deny that strange things appear to happen. Witnesses are convinced that they have seen men walk across fires without being burnt. Some people are certain that their dreams predict the future. Others believe that they can communicate with the dead.

However, the fact that such things *appear* to happen does not mean that they actually do. It is well known that people often believe what they want to believe. There is also the problem of trickery.

Scientists state, quite correctly, that for an unusual gift, such as ESP, to be accepted, it must be proved beyond doubt. This would involve a series of experiments which are properly supervised so that no trickery can be carried out. The results of the experiments would then be analysed.

Many experiments have been carried out on all the supernatural phenomena mentioned in this book. Some of the results indicate that the strange powers people possess may be genuine; other results are less impressive.

However, none of these experiments has been accepted as proof by scientists. Sometimes the experts have pointed out errors in the experiment itself. On other occasions they have criticized the researchers, sometimes accusing *them* of trickery. The most common scientific reaction to research into supernatural mysteries appears to be total disbelief. Because such strange events do not fit into established theories, scientists think that they cannot happen. It is worth remembering that 200 years ago, electric light bulbs and cookers would not have fitted scientific ideas then current.

Perhaps in the future, scientists will be forced to change their ideas and accept ESP, foretelling the future and dowsing. Or perhaps the scientists are correct when they say that such things do not happen. What do you think?

This tangle of bent paperclips, in a sealed glass container, was created by telekinesis. With such evidence available, can scientists continue to doubt that supernatural powers exist?

Glossary

Archaeologist A person who studies ancient remains which have been found in the ground.

Bizarre Strange; very unusual.

Clairvoyant Someone who can see into the future or past.

Congregation All the people attending a church service.

Controversial Something that causes a lot of disagreement.

Dowsing The ability to find buried objects by using a bit of wood, two metal rods or a pendulum. A person who finds things in this way is called a dowser.

ESP The initials of Extra Sensory Perception, which is the ability to detect things without using the normal senses of touch, taste, sight, hearing or smell.

Fast A period of time spent without eating.

Fiction An imaginary or untrue occurrence; the opposite of fact.

Figment Something that does not exist except in a person's imagination.

Genuine Real.

Imagery Using one phrase to mean another, such as calling the sea 'the whales' home'.

Inflation A period of time when money becomes worth less and goods cost more to buy.

Levitation The ability to float in the air.

Ley line An imaginary straight line which connects places of religious or ancient importance.

Meditate To think deeply.

Medium A person who claims to be able to communicate with the dead.

Muslim A follower of Islam.

Phenomenon A remarkable or unusual event.

Prediction The act of stating that an event will happen before it actually does.

Premonition The feeling that a certain event is about to occur.

Prophet A person who makes predictions.

Psychic Another name for a medium.

Sceptics People who doubt the truth about something.

Seamstress A woman who earns her living by sewing and making clothes.

Seance A meeting with a medium where people try to communicate with the dead.

Soul The invisible part of a person that some people believe goes on living after death.

Spirit Another name for the soul.

Spiritualism The belief that souls can communicate with living people.

TK Short for telekinesis, which is the ability to move objects by thought-power alone.

Trance To concentrate on something so strongly that you are unaware of what is going on around you.

Further reading

Brett, Bernard, *The Hamlyn Book of Mysteries* (Hamlyn, 1986)

Holiday, Ted, *The Goblin Universe* (Llewellyn, 1988)

Innes, Brian (ed), *The Unexplained* (Orbis, 1982)

Supernatural World Omnibus (Usborne, 1986)

Index

Picture Acknowledgements

The publishers would like to thank the following for supplying illustrations for this book: David Cumming 6, 43; Mary Evans Picture Library 7 (upper), 24 (upper), 30 (upper: *Psychic News*), 31, 37 (upper); Fortean Picture Library 7 (lower: Dr J T Richards), 10 (Dr J T Richards), 37 (lower: Paul Broadhurst), 46 (Dennis Stacy); Macdonald/Aldus 24 (lower), 28, 44; Ronald Sheridan 21; TOPHAM 11, 13, 18, 20, 26.